Clocks and calendars timeline

c. 30,000 BC–15,000 BC

Prehistoric hunters in Europe make the first known calendars.

c. 1300 AD

Early mechanical clocks are made in Europe.

3114 BC

Maya and other peoples of Central America measured time using a calendar from this date.

c. 3500 BC–1500 BC

Ancient Egyptians invent sundials and water-clocks.

c. 1450–1550

Locksmiths in Germany invent clocks powered by springs, and make the first watches.

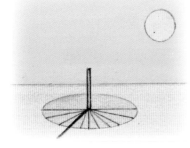

c. 500 BC

In Asia and Europe, candles begin to be used for measuring time.

1949

Super-accurate atomic clock invented by Isidor Rabi in the United States.

1884

Greenwich Meridian (imaginary line) chosen as starting-point for measuring time all round the world.

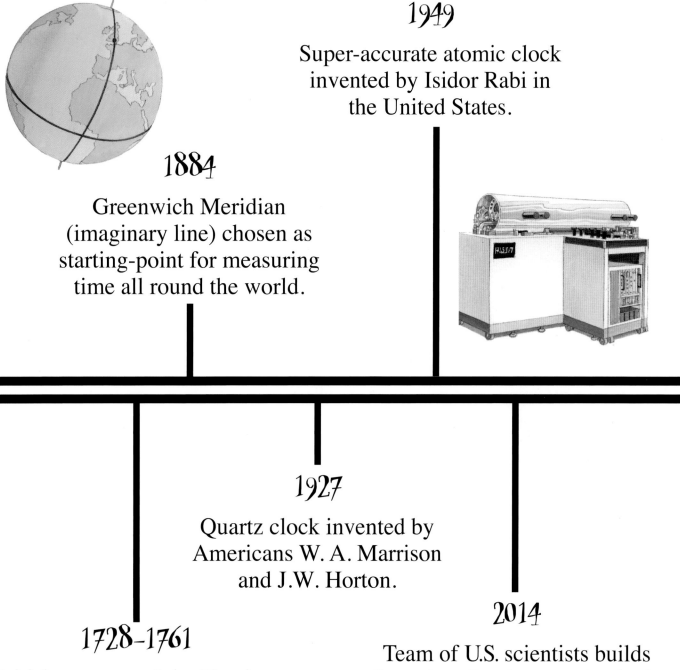

1927

Quartz clock invented by Americans W. A. Marrison and J.W. Horton.

2014

Team of U.S. scientists builds Strontium Lattice atomic clock. It is predicted to keep perfect time for 5 billion years.

1728–1761

British carpenter John Harrison invents chronometers, to keep accurate time on long voyages.

Calendars round the world

Our calendar's based on the...

...Sun!

...Moon!

...Sun and Moon!

Ancient Egyptians, Athenians

Arabs, Muslims

Ancient Chinese, Jews

...Sun, Moon and planet Venus!

Clocks and watches show us time passing, but calendars are ways of organising time. They measure, record and predict time past, present and future. Calendars can be written down, carved in stone, programmed on computers, or stored in people's memories.

At different times and in different places, people invented all kinds of calendars. Some were based on observations of the Sun, Moon, planets and stars. Some followed the seasons of the year. Some counted time from important events. Many were based on religious beliefs, myths and legends.

Aztec Calendar Stone, Central America, c. 1500 CE

Author:

Fiona Macdonald studied history at Cambridge University, England, and at the University of East Anglia. She has taught in schools, adult education and universities, and is the author of numerous books for children on historical topics.

Artist:

David Antram was born in Brighton, England, in 1958. He studied at Eastbourne College of Art and then worked in advertising for 15 years before becoming a full-time artist. He has illustrated many children's non-fiction books.

Series creator:

David Salariya was born in Dundee, Scotland. He has illustrated a wide range of books and has created and designed many new series for publishers in the UK and overseas. David established The Salariya Book Company in 1989. He lives in Brighton with his wife, illustrator Shirley Willis, and their son Jonathan.

Editor: **Caroline Coleman**

Editorial Assistant: **Mark Williams**

Published in Great Britain in MMXVI by
Book House, an imprint of
The Salariya Book Company Ltd
25 Marlborough Place, Brighton BN1 1UB
www.salariya.com
www.book-house.co.uk
ISBN: 978-1-910184-91-2

S A L A R I Y A

3 5 7 9 8 6 4 2

A CIP catalogue record for this book is available from the British Library.

Printed and bound in China.
Reprinted in MMXVII.

Visit
www.salariya.com
for our online catalogue and
free fun stuff.

PAPER FROM
SUSTAINABLE
FORESTS

You Wouldn't Want to Live Without™

Clocks and Calendars!

Written by
Fiona Macdonald

Illustrated by
David Antram

Series created by
David Salariya

BOOK HOUSE
a SALARIYA *imprint*

Contents

Introduction

Imagine, if you can, a world without clocks and calendars. Where no one knew what time it was, which day of the week, or even which year! Buses, trains and planes would run late, shops would not know when to open, and school classes could not begin or end on time. There would be no holidays, no festivals – and no birthdays. You would not even know how old you were! It's fortunate that for the past 30,000 years – maybe longer – clever men and women have worked out ways to measure and keep track of time, using many different clocks and calendars. We owe them all a big 'thank you!' Read on, and find out more…

Most people nowadays might not know what this ancient timekeeping device is, or how to use it. But these old-fashioned sundials paved the way for clocks as we know them today.

Years and seasons

You're a Stone Age hunter. You survive by killing buffalo that run past your camp every summer. You store the meat carefully, to make it last all winter. But by springtime, you're hungry, and need to know when the buffalo will return. You look for clues that summer's coming: green grass growing, longer daylight hours, changing stars in the sky. Once these appear, the buffalo should come back again. You remember this knowledge, and make drawings and carvings to record it. Congratulations! You've invented the world's first calendar!

Waaah! I want my dinner!

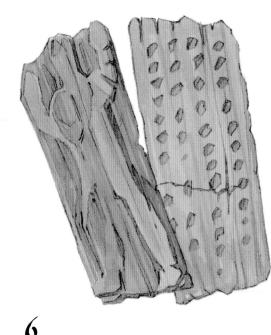

SIGN OF THE TIMES. The oldest surviving calendar, carved on mammoth tusk more than 30,000 years ago, shows the constellation Orion (left) and a nine-month pregnancy timetable (right).

STAR-SPOTTERS. The ancient Borana calendar from East Africa was based on observing the Moon and seven special stars. It is accurate, and is still used today.

Too late! Missed them!

Top tip

Look out for clues to the changing seasons of the year: migrating birds, blossoming flowers, high tides and river floods!

PREHISTORIC PUZZLE.
The Stone Circle at Callanish, Isle of Lewis, Scotland, was built c. 3000 BC, as a calendar, or a temple, or a tomb.

CACTUS CALENDAR.
Before paper was invented, Native American peoples recorded important events on calendar sticks made of dried cactus.

Months, weeks, days, hours...

Whose day is it anyway?

EGYPTIANS say that each new day starts at dawn.

BABYLONIANS, Greeks, Jews and Muslims believe that days start at nightfall.

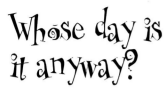ast forward several thousand years to 1500 BC. Now calendars are more complicated, and each civilisation has its own. Babylonians list 30 days in a month, 12 months in a year and 24 hours in a day. Jewish calendars have weeks of seven days. Egyptian years last for 360 days plus five 'extras'. Today, we still use these ancient calendars to plan our busy lives, but many other old ways of organising time have almost been forgotten. How would you like to follow these calendar traditions: weeks with 4 days (Africa), days with 10 hours (China) and years with 18 months (Central America)?

ANCIENT ROMAN and Chinese days would start at midnight.

MAYA AND AZTEC days began at noon, when the Sun was highest in the sky.

Cockadoodledoo

FARMERS' days began when roosters started crowing. The noise made it hard to sleep.

The first time machines

HANDY! Keep track of time like an ancient Egyptian: divide daylight into 12 hours. That way, you can count them on one hand. It's easy – try it!

3 joints

$3 \times 4 = 12$

4 fingers

See! It's very simple, just a stick and a half-circle dial carved on stone. But it tells the time for all to see, so long as the Sun is shining. It's a sundial – the world's first time-measuring machine. Sundials were invented in ancient Egypt around 5,500 years ago and are still used today. They work by casting a shadow. From dawn to dusk, as the Sun seems to move across the sky, the shadow moves as well, pointing to the hours marked on the dial.

How to read a sundial

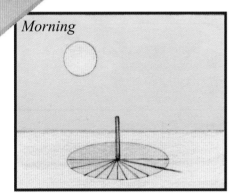

Morning

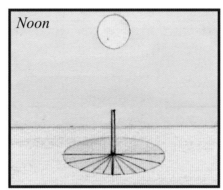

Noon

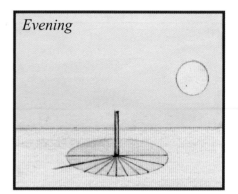

Evening

THE SUN appears low in the sky. Its slanting light casts a long shadow that moves around from the start of the dial.

THE SUN appears high overhead. Its light casts a short, strong shadow right on the mid-point of the dial.

THE SUN appears to sink down. The sundial shadow grows longer and moves towards the end point of the dial.

Go with the Flow

Wonderful water?

WATER-CLOCKS usually work well – but not always. They need a steady flow of water.

Time never stands still! That's why the first clockmakers, in Greece, Egypt, Asia and America, use substances that move at a regular rate to measure time. Most choose flowing water; others prefer sand or mercury (a liquid metal). They all know that a fixed amount of their chosen substance will always take the same time to run from one place to another. Let's visit Greece around 350 BC to see a clepsydra (water clock) in action! Water clocks are used to time speeches at Greek assemblies – an essential part of democracy!

WATER PRESSURE is also important.

THEY also need to have regular repairs.

FREEZING winters can cause problems.

AND regular clock time does not match time measured by the Sun!

Now they tell me! It's a clock!

Make holes in a plastic pot. (Ask an adult for help.) Put it in a bowl of water, then time how long it takes to fill and sink. Now you can use it as a water clock!

IN ANCIENT PERSIA (Iran) clocks are bowls with holes. If you drop one into water, it always takes the same time to sink.

Stopped by the clock! What a wonderful invention!

Blowing in the wind

Don't want a water clock? Then how about a candle? They burn at a slow, steady rate, ideal for measuring time. They're simple to use, and light to carry. Unlike sundials, they work indoors and in the dark, as well. Since around AD 500, they've been replacing old-style oil lamps, which people have used for centuries. But candles aren't cheap. They drip. They don't burn for long. They can cause fires. They can't tell the exact time – not even whether it's morning or afternoon. And if the flame blows out, they're useless!

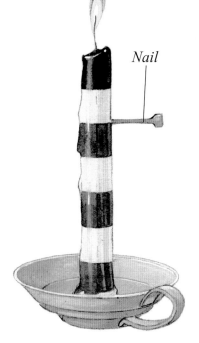

Nail

ROYAL REMINDER.
England's King Alfred (AD 849–899) turned candles into alarm-clocks by adding nails. As the wax burned, the nails fell out and woke him.

SWEET AND SLOW.
In Asia, precious incense burned slowly and gently and was used to measure time. It smelled good, too!

TIME FLIES!
Hourglasses filled with trickling sand were safer than burning lamps or candles. They were good timekeepers, except on ships in a storm!

Oh no! How will we know when it's dinner time?!

A tishoo!

Need to measure time precisely? Then ask Arab mathematician Al-Battani. Around AD 900, he proved that a year has 365 days, 5 hours, 46 minutes and 24 seconds. This varies only very slightly from what we know to be true today.

Four o'clock and all's well!

LOST YOUR LIGHT? Then listen for the night watchman. He tells people when to go to bed, and when to get up again.

SAY YOUR PRAYERS –
it's a good way of counting time. Old books told cooks which prayer was best for each recipe.

15

Round and round

It's the year 1300 in Europe, and there's been a timekeeping revolution. We've got mechanical clocks! Look, high on that tower, a clock face made of metal! Now, see that heavy weight? Slowly, steadily, it's being pulled down by gravity. It's linked by a rope to wheels and gears. As the weight sinks down, the gears move a metal rod. That turns another wheel and it moves the clock hand round the dial. When the weight reaches the ground, strong men wind it back to the top of the tower. Excellent engineering!

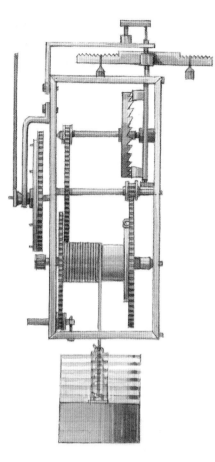

TEETH AND TIME.
The toothed wheel turns; the rod moves the balance wheel; the balance wheel moves the clock hand.

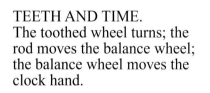

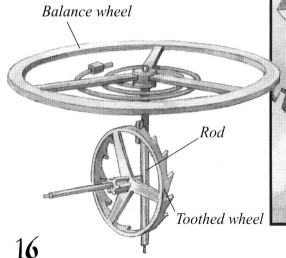

Balance wheel

Rod

Toothed wheel

WEIGHT AND POWER.
Mechanical clocks are powered by weights of metal or stone. Weights need to be carefully balanced, or the clock will run fast or slow.

GEAR UP! Mechanical clocks measure time by a steady flow of little movements. These are controlled and transmitted by notched wheels, called gears.

16

Prague astronomical clock, c. 1410

How it works

Q. Our word 'clock' comes from an old French word, 'cloche', meaning 'bell'. Can you guess why?

A. Before mechanical clocks were invented monks rang church bells to announce prayer time.

TICK-TOCK

Mechanical clocks have brought a new sound to the world: a steady 'tick-tock' that tells everyone time is passing.

Clang!

These new clocks are very noisy neighbours!

Side to side

Swoosh! Swoosh! The sound of genius! We're in Italy, it's 1641, and brilliant mathematician Galileo Galilei has just designed a clock with a pendulum. That's a weight swinging from side to side: another regular, steady movement useful for measuring time. Galileo's clock will never be built, but his studies will inspire a great Dutch scientist, Christiaan Huygens, to create the first pendulum clock in 1657. Pendulum clocks are so accurate – and look so grand – that all rich Europeans want one! They're the best timekeepers invented so far.

LIGHT FANTASTIC. Galileo observed a heavy church lamp swinging from side to side. Each swing was the same length, and took an equal amount of time.

MODERN MODEL of a clock based on Galileo's 1641 design (below).

Pendulum

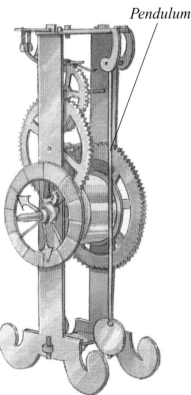

BY THE 1500s, the Christian Calendar is no longer accurate, so Pope Gregory XIII introduces a new calendar in 1582. There are riots, because Gregory's calendar 'loses' 11 days – people want them back!

MINUTES (60 per hour) and seconds (60 per minute) begin to be widely used in timekeeping from around 1500. Soon, clocks are fitted with minute hands. Second hands are added later, around 1780.

You can take it with you

Let's stay in early modern Europe for a while, because it's home to yet another clever timekeeping invention. Around 1450, expert metalworkers in Germany began to make locks that opened with keys that unwound a spring. After several accidents – springs can be dangerous! – they realised that the energy stored in a coiled spring can also be used for timekeeping. If the spring unwinds gently and steadily, it can measure time and turn the hands of a clock. Springs are small, so spring-powered clocks can be light and portable. Now, around 1550, they're the world's first watches!

Spring

SIMPLE BUT POWERFUL. A coil spring is a length of wire wound into a spiral (left). Springs store energy, then release it as they unwind.

WATCH THIS! Springs wound with a key were used to turn wheels, gears and balance wheels (see page 16), and move the hands of clocks.

Gears

Hour hand

Spring

Key

Minute hand

Think of it as a surprise gift, your Majesty!

You can do it!

Coil a safe pipe-cleaner into a spring, then hold it between your fingertips. Can you feel the stored energy in the spring pushing against them?

DON'T BE LATE. Without a watch, you'll find it difficult to check the time when you are out and about, in town or in the country.

TIME FOR ACTION. Soldiers, synchronise your watches! After about 1900, cheap watches worn by troops made battle planning easier.

STATUS SYMBOL. A fine pocket watch with a fancy gold chain showed that the wearer was well organised, up-to-date, and wealthy.

Time around the world

You're a traveller or explorer, far out at sea or in the middle of a desert. And you're lost! You can estimate your position north or south from the angle of the Sun. But east or west? That's hopeless! What you need is an ultra-reliable clock – a chronometer. Set the chronometer to the right time when you start your journey. Then, as you travel, see what time the chronometer shows at noon when the Sun is highest in the sky. The difference between chronometer time and local time, measured by the Sun, will let you calculate how far east or west you've travelled.

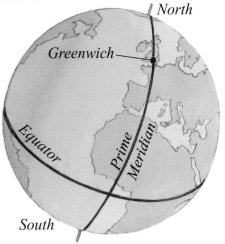

TIME LINE. In 1884 governments agreed to measure world time starting from a Meridian (imaginary line) passing through Greenwich, England.

Clock time!

Sun time!

LOCAL TIME, measured by the Sun, changes by one hour for every 15 degrees travelled east or west. But time that is measured by clocks stays the same.

ENGLISH carpenter John Harrison spent over 30 years (1728–1761) perfecting his spring-powered chronometers. They kept excellent time, even on long sea voyages.

EARLY RAILWAYS had a problem: different local times! 'Railway time', using just one clock for a whole rail network, began in Britain from 1840.

You can do it!

Be a virtual time-traveller! Using the Internet or a library, can you find out what time it is in New York when it is noon in your home town?

That can't be the 8:38?

TRAVEL TIME DISASTER! In 1853, two American passenger trains collided because the guards had set their watches to different local times in their home towns.

Clockwatching!

Are you a good time-keeper? If so, would you like to live around 1900, in a busy, dirty city in Europe or the United States? You'll see clocks all around: in stations, shops, offices and factories. That's because workers must arrive on time, and not waste a second idling! Tight time-schedules also make sure that factory machines run smoothly. Away from work, clocks will soon become part of twentieth-century life, for everyone. War and peace, medicine, technology, sport and entertainment will be unthinkable without them.

Top tip

Get organised! Learn to manage your time! You can start by making a list. It might contain urgent tasks to finish, new books to read – or your future ambitions.

MEDIA TIME. Have you heard them? Time signals at the start of television and radio broadcasts.

SPORTS TIME. Old-style stop-watches and modern digital clocks time record-breaking races.

LIFE-TIME. Medical monitors use timers to check your pulse, heartbeat, and other signs of life.

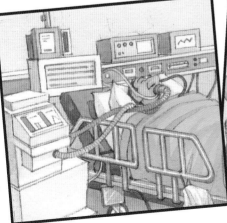

SPACE TIME. Rocket launches and space flights rely on clocks for split-second timing.

WORKING TO TIME. Timers can control tasks performed by automatic robots.

25

Just a minute...

Pendulum clocks are good, chronometers are better – but twentieth-century inventions have changed timekeeping forever. Quartz clocks (1927) and atomic clocks (1949) still use steady, repeated movements to measure time. But now these movements are superfast: atoms in an atomic clock 'flip' 9,192,631,770 times per second!! Atomic clocks are extraordinarily accurate, but quartz clocks are amazing in a different way. They're so cheap to mass-produce that most electronic devices are fitted with one. How many can you spot in your home or school?

DO YOU WEAR a quartz watch? If so, it works this way. Electric current from a battery (1) makes a quartz crystal (2) vibrate 32,768 times per second.

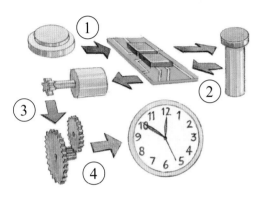

THE VIBRATION powers a tiny electric motor (3). This turns gears and wheels (4), and they measure time and move the watch hands.

STAY RIGHT ON TIME. Signals from atomic clocks control timekeeping devices in computers, phones and GPS systems all round the world.

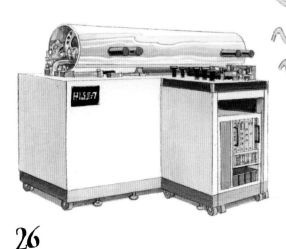

You can do it!

Check your watch or clock against atomic time! You can see live signals from a U.S. Navy atomic clock on the U.S. Naval Observatory website: http://tycho.usno.navy.mil/simpletime.html

$$E = MC^2$$

STRANGE BUT TRUE. Atomic clocks helped investigate time itself. In experiments on jet planes in 1971, they tested a theory (above) from scientist Albert Einstein (1879–1955).

EINSTEIN was right! Atomic clocks proved that time does not pass steadily, but speeds up or slows down, depending on how fast we are moving.

Time rules, O.K.?

Today, almost everything we do is timed to the last minute. And we like to do it quickly! For working, studying, eating, playing, downloading data, or just messaging friends, fast is fantastic! In many ways, that's great. There's so much to achieve and enjoy, if we can organise our time. But, just sometimes, it can seem as if clever timekeeping devices are ruling our lives.

Dear reader, if you could choose, which would you prefer: fast-paced modern life, or a world without clocks and calendars?

Relaxing time

Dinner time

Homework time

Sports time

Tick tock

Music time

DEAR DIARY. Do you keep a diary? If so, why? To record your secret thoughts, like people in the past, or to plan your busy life?

IN CONTROL? There's nothing like a timetable to organise work, travel and holidays. But too much information can sometimes be troublesome…

Alligator clips with leads

Big potato

Copper wire

Galvanised nails

11:57

1.5V battery-powered clock, battery removed

Follow this diagram (above) to make your own potato-powered clock.

Brrrïïnnng!

Breakfast time

School time

Bus time

Lunchtime

NON-STOP CLOCK.
The 24-hour clock was designed around AD 1400, in Italy. Now it's used worldwide, for travel, in hospitals and by armed forces, to avoid dangerous confusion.

14:32

MOST DIGITAL CLOCKS
and timers don't have traditional 'analogue' (round, 12-hour) clock faces. Instead, they show the 24-hour clock in clear, simple numbers.

Glossary

Analogue clock A timekeeping machine with a round face (dial) and either 12 or 24 numerals.

Atomic clock A clock that uses very rapidly changing states of energy in atoms to measure time.

Atoms Tiny particles, the smallest 'building blocks' of matter. Everything in the world is made of them. There are 90 different natural atoms; scientists have created around 28 more.

Babylonian Belonging to a civilisation based in ancient Babylon that reached the peak of its power around 1780 BC.

Chronometer A very accurate clock or watch, originally designed for timekeeping and navigation at sea.

Clepsydra The ancient Greek name for a water clock. It means 'water thief'.

Clock time Time measured at a regular, unchanging rate by a watch or clock.

Constellation A pattern of stars in the night sky. Ancient peoples gave them names.

Dial A flat circle or half circle, with divisions of time marked on it.

Flip (in atomic clocks) When parts of atoms change from one energy state to another.

Galvanised Coated with a thin layer of zinc (a shiny grey metal) for protection.

Gears Wheels with notches or 'teeth' around the rim. They transmit force or movement from one part of a machine to another.

Gravity A natural force that pulls objects toward one another. For example, Earth's gravity pulls all objects that are less massive (contain less matter) towards it.

Incense Resin (gum from trees) and other natural substances that produce sweet-smelling smoke when they are burned. Often used in religious ceremonies.

Local time Time measured by observation of the Sun. Unlike **clock time**, local time changes as we travel east or west around the world.

Meridian Imaginary line drawn around the Earth, passing through the North and South Poles.

Metronome Simple pendulum clock, used by musicians to keep time. The centre of mass of the pendulum can be adjusted so that it beats faster or slower.

Observation Careful looking, measuring and recording.

Olympiad A period of four years, starting from 776 BC (the legendary date of the first Olympic Games). It was used to count years in ancient Greece.

Pendulum A weight hanging from a fixed point so it can swing freely from back to front or side to side.

Quartz Silicon dioxide; a very common white mineral found as crystals in the earth.

Railway time Standardised time used by a whole railway network, for safety and to avoid confusion.

Transmit Carry, pass along.

Tusk An overgrown tooth. Mammoth tusks could grow 5 metres long.

Vibration Shaking. Regular vibrations are sometimes used to measure time, e.g. in quartz watches.

Index

Keeping time

Two of the world's most popular activities, sport and music, depend on accurate timekeeping.

- A close-run thing. The time difference between top athletes in a race can be less than $\frac{1}{100}$ of a second. That's much, much less time than it takes to say 'clock' or 'calendar'.

- Joint decision. Quartz clocks used at Olympic competitions can measure $\frac{1}{1000}$ of a second. But at the 1984 Los Angeles Olympics, two female swimmers were both declared winners. No one could measure any difference in time between them.

- Gooooaaaal! Extra time for injuries or stoppages can make all the difference to a soccer match. In the UEFA Super Cup Final, 2013, both teams scored last-minute goals in the final extra moments. The winner (Bayern Munich) was eventually decided by a penalty shoot-out.

- All together. Members of bands and orchestras learn to play in time with one another. They practice with a metronome and read the composer's time indication on sheet music. At a concert, they are guided by a conductor and watch or listen for signals from each other.

- Feel the beat! To put extra emotion into their music, singers and instrumentalists often squeeze or stretch time. This can ruin a live performance – or make it extra exciting.

Top clocks

- The world's most accurate clock is the Strontium Lattice Clock, made at the U.S. Joint Institute for Laboratory Astrophysics in 2014. The atoms inside flick 430 trillion times per second. It is predicted to keep perfect time for 5 billion years.

- The world's most expensive man's watch was sold in 2014 for £13.4 million ($24.4 million U.S. dollars). Crafted from real gold, the 'Graves Supercomplication' model was designed for a U.S. businessman. The most expensive woman's watch is the Chopard 201, which features 874 different coloured diamonds, and costs £16.6 million ($25 million U.S. dollars).

- The Omega Speedmaster Professional is the only watch to have been worn on the Moon, by U.S. astronaut Buzz Aldrin in 1969.

- In 2012, the Rolex Deepsea Challenge watch set a new record for underwater timekeeping when it was carried 10,908 m (35,787 ft) below the sea surface, and worked well!

- The oldest clock still working is probably the astronomical clock at Salisbury Cathedral, England (though clocks in France and Italy also claim this record). It was made around 1386 and still keeps good time.

Did you know?

- Around 250 BC, the ancient Greeks invented 'calling' clocks that told the time by hooting like an owl. Modern cuckoo-clocks (first made in Germany around 1600) copy this idea.

- The Samrat Yantra, Jaipur, India, is the world's largest sundial. It was build in 1728 and is 27 metres (90 ft) high.

- The two most famous clocks in the world are the Grand Central Terminal Clock in New York, built in 1913; and 'Big Ben', a huge bell that rings out the time in the tall tower clock at the Houses of Parliament in London, built in 1859.

- The world's tallest clock tower is in Mecca, Saudi Arabia. It is 601 m (1,972 ft) high. As well as telling the time, it also broadcasts the Muslim call to prayer five times a day.

- In 1999, the first prototype (working model) Long Now Clock started ticking. Long Now Clocks are designed to run for 10,000 years, and to make people think about their own short existence, and long-term time, in a new way.

- Although twenty-first century planes, trains, computers and the media all rely on the same international calendar, people still use over 40 ancient ways of recording and planning time. These include Jewish and Muslim religious calendars, and traditional calendars from China and Central America.

- We can never travel back in time, but time travel to the future is scientifically possible. If it ever becomes popular, we are going to need new kinds of clocks and calendars!

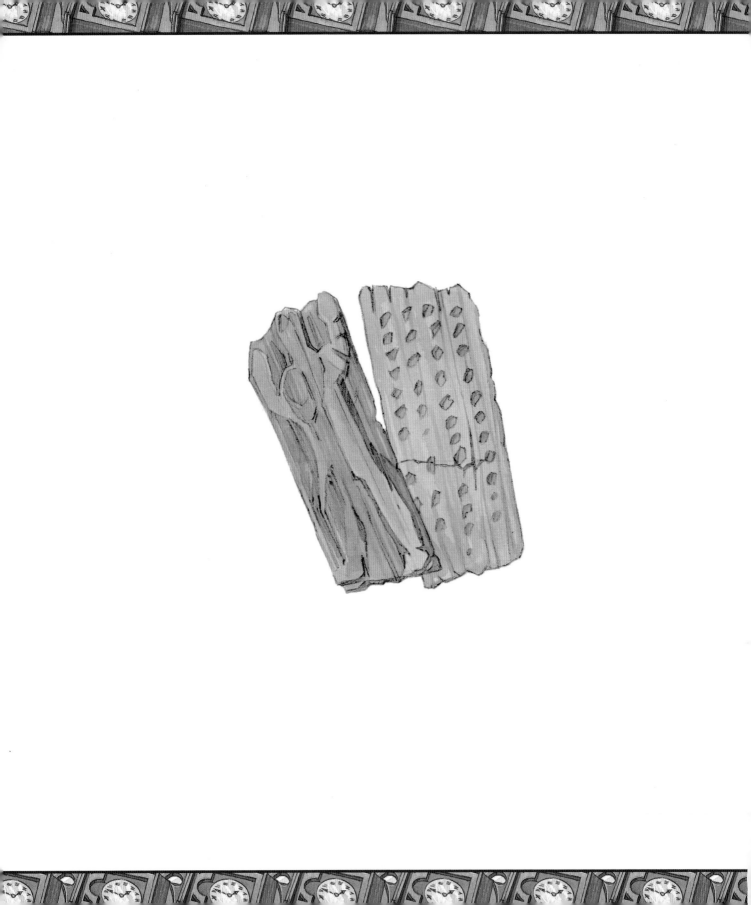